# Muhammad

## Prophet of Islam

Jessica Cohn, M.S.

## Publishing Credits

Dona Herweck Rice, *Editor-in-Chief*
Lee Aucoin, *Creative Director*
Torrey Maloof, *Editor*
Neri Garcia, *Senior Designer*
Stephanie Reid, *Photo Researcher*
Rachelle Cracchiolo, M.S.Ed., *Publisher*

## Image Credits

cover Bridgeman Art Library; p.4 North Wind Picture Archives/Alamy; p.5 The Granger Collection; p.6 (top) Bridgeman Art Library, p.6 (bottom) Corbis; p.7 (left) The Granger Collection, p.7 (right) Shutterstock, Inc.; p.8 Alamy; p.9 Bridgeman Art Library; p.10 Getty Images; p.11 (top) Newscom, p.11 (bottom) Getty Images; p.12 Bridgeman Art Library; p.13 The Granger Collection; p.14 Newscom; p.15 The Granger Collection; p.17 Bridgeman Art Library; p.18 Bridgeman Art Library, p.19 Getty Images; p.20 Bridgeman Art Library; p.21 The Granger Collection; p.22 Getty Images; p.23 (top) Bridgeman Art Library, p.23 (bottom) Bridgeman Art Library; p.24 Bridgeman Art Library; p.25 (left) The Granger Collection, p.25 (right) Getty Images; p.27 (top left) Bridgeman Art Library, p.27 (top right) Bridgeman Art Library, p.27 (bottom) Corbis; p.28 Alamy; p.29 Newscom; p.32 (background) Shutterstock, Inc., p.32 (top) Newscom; back cover Getty Images

---

**Teacher Created Materials**
5301 Oceanus Drive
Huntington Beach, CA 92649-1030
http://www.tcmpub.com

**ISBN 978-1-4333-5004-7**

Printed in China
Nordica.082019.CA21901100

# Table of Contents

# Early Years

## Arabia

Life was hard. There were no schools. The people in charge were the leaders of family groups. They made decisions that favored their own families. The people raised animals, made goods, traded goods, or stole them. It was a lawless time. This was Arabia (uh-REY-bee-uh) during the sixth century.

Arabia is a **peninsula**. A peninsula is a narrow piece of land that sticks out into the water. Arabia is located in Asia next to Africa. This desert land served as a bridge for the people of the East. The empires around it were often at war.

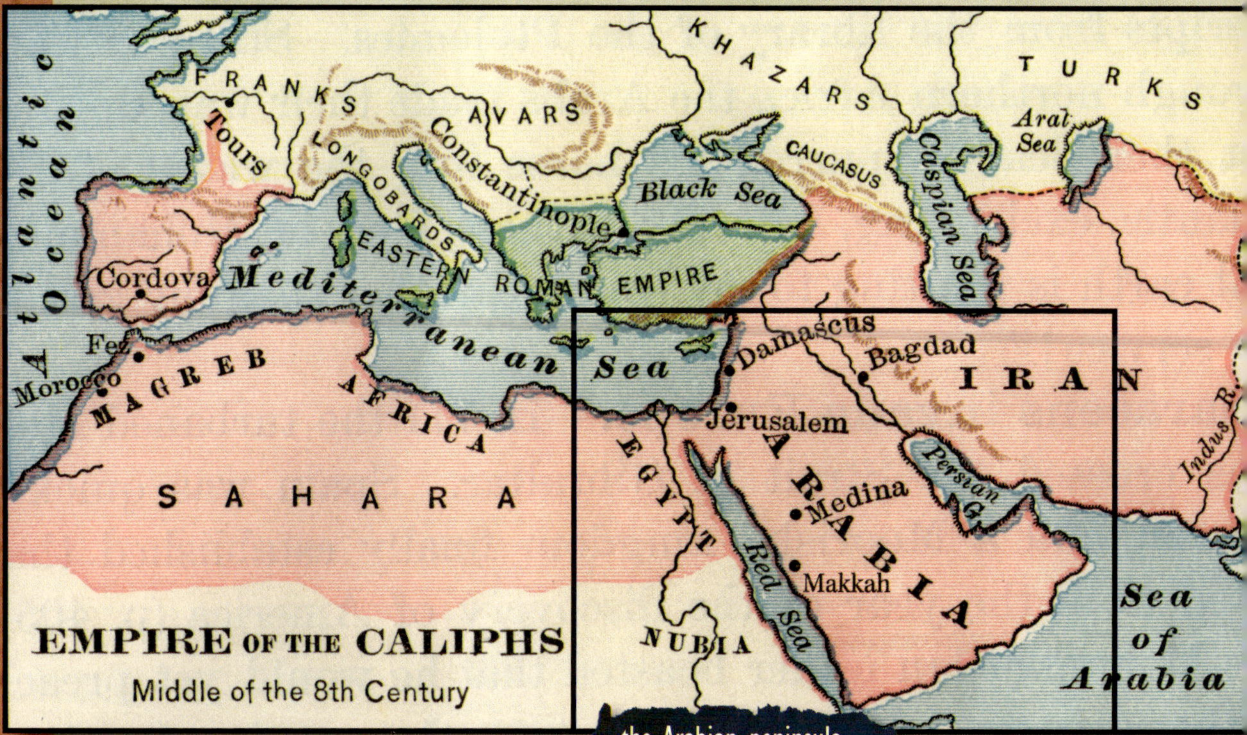


the Arabian peninsula

Muhammad builds a small mosque in Medina.

The big towns in Arabia were Medina and Makkah (MAH-kuh). Muhammad (moh-HAHM-uhd) was born in Makkah in AD 570. Life was hard. Young Muhammad was sometimes treated as an outsider. Even though he struggled to fit in, Muhammad would grow to be the founder of the religion known as **Islam** (is-LAWM).

Today, Arabia is known as Saudi Arabia, and Makkah is the center of Islam. Islam has spread all around the world, and Muhammad has become a key figure in its history.

## Makkah or Mecca

Some **Muslims**, or followers of Islam, call their holy city Makkah instead of Mecca (MEH-kuh). *Mecca* has come to mean "the center of activity" in Western culture. For example, people may call a city a "shopping mecca" if it has a lot of shopping malls. Often, Muslims do not like the name of their holy city used out of context, so they use *Makkah* instead.

## Muhammad or Mohammed

There is only one true way to spell *Muhammad* in the Arabic language. However, when translated into English, *Muhammad* is spelled in many different ways. *Mohammed*, *Mohammad*, *Mohamed*, and *Mahamed* are just a few.

Prophet Muhammad

## No Face?

In Islam, picturing Muhammad is wrong. However, some people think his face can be shown as a blank. Others think it is okay to show him with a veil. Covering Muhammad's face is to remind people to worship only God, not humans.

## Before Islam

Before Islam, people in Arabia believed in many gods. Each tribe had a god. There were animal gods and gods for things like luck. People believed that evil spirits roamed the desert at night. People would wear charms to guard against the evil spirits.

## Muhammad's Family

In Muhammad's society, clans were very important. A clan is a group of families. These groups reach far beyond a mother, a father, and a child. The cousins of cousins can be included. The people in a clan can look back in time and find **ancestors**, or relatives, that they share.

Muhammad's clan had ties to other clans. Together, they formed larger groups called *tribes*. However, the ties among the tribes were often broken. Though the clans had rules, it was overall a lawless time. The clans attacked and stole belongings. They even stole people from one another. Upholding the honor of the clan remained important no matter what happened among the tribes.

God speaks to Abraham.

the Ka'ba in Makkah then

the Ka'ba in Makkah now

Muhammad's family was connected to the ruling tribe of Makkah. The clan was called the Hashim (HA-sheem), for a man by that same name. The Hashim guarded the **Ka'ba** (KAH-buh). That was, and continues to be, the main **shrine** in Makkah. Muhammad's tribe was called the Quraysh (koo-REYSCH). The tribe's roots can be traced back to Ishmael. He was a son of Abraham. Abraham is known in Islam, Judaism, and Christianity as the leader who first said there was only one God.

## Muhammad's Upbringing

Muhammad was born into an important clan. However, this did not protect him from a troublesome childhood. Muhammad's father died on a trip before Muhammad was born. After his father's death, Muhammad's grandfather and mother were in charge of raising him.

Most historians say that Muhammad's grandfather sent him as a baby to be cared for by the **Bedouins** (BED-oo-inz) in the desert. They were **herders** who lived a simple life outside the towns. They moved from place to place with their animals. It was considered a healthy life.

### Year of the Elephant

Just before Muhammad was born, an army tried to conquer Makkah. The soldiers came from what is now Ethiopia (ee-thee-OH-pee-uh). They had an elephant. In many stories, the creature bowed down before reaching Makkah, and their mission failed. People connect this event to Muhammad's birth as a signal he had saved the city.

### Life in the Desert

As a baby, Muhammad was sent to the desert. This was an Arab custom. People who could afford it sent their children to herders to grow strong and learn about self-control. The children were expected to gain a sense of independence and dignity.

Bedouin camp

A woman named Halimah (HA-lee-muh) took care of Muhammad. When Muhammad was older, Halimah took him back to his mother's home, but it was not a long reunion. Muhammad's mother died when he was about six years old. Not long after that, his grandfather died, and Muhammad became an orphan.

One of Muhammad's uncles was put in charge of the clan. The clan worked as traders. Muhammad learned how to buy and sell goods. While working as a trader, the boy's future took root in the sands.

# Time to Think

## A Family of His Own

As a trader, Muhammad earned a **reputation** for being smart and honest. Muhammad was known for his kindness as well. When he was a young man, a woman named Khadijah (kah-DEE-juh) hired Muhammad to run her business. She was known for being rich and caring.

Muhammad marries Khadijah.

In time, Khadijah asked Muhammad to marry her. They were together for more than 20 years. The accounts of how many children they had differ. Most historians believe the couple had four daughters and two sons. Much like his childhood, Muhammad's family life was marked by death. His sons died young. Only one of Muhammad's children would outlive him.

As Muhammad entered middle age, he began to think about his place in the world. He had always felt like an outsider. As he grew older, Muhammad was concerned about other outsiders and the poor. He was unhappy with the way the world worked.

Muhammad started to seek time alone, where he could think about things in a serious manner. Khadijah supported his decision to explore and think about the meaning of life.

visitors to the cave on Hira

## The Cave

As Muhammad grew tired of the ways of the world, he started to travel alone to a cave. The cave was located outside of Makkah on a mountain called Hira (HE-rah). It was there that Muhammad first had visions of an angel. The angel was Gabriel. According to the story of Islam, Gabriel told Muhammad that he had been chosen for special work.

## Only Child

The only child of Muhammad's first family who outlived him was his daughter Fatimah (FAH-tee-mah). She is a key figure in the Islamic faith. Muslims view Fatimah as a role model for all Muslim women.

The angel Gabriel visits Muhammad in the cave.

## Visited by Angels

In the story of Islam, Muhammad began speaking with angels when he was about 40 years old. An angel named Gabriel was the first to appear. It was the year 610. Muhammad was in a cave outside Makkah, thinking about the issues that troubled him. The angel appeared and told him that there was one God. He said that Muhammad was the messenger for God.

Gabriel visits Muhammad.

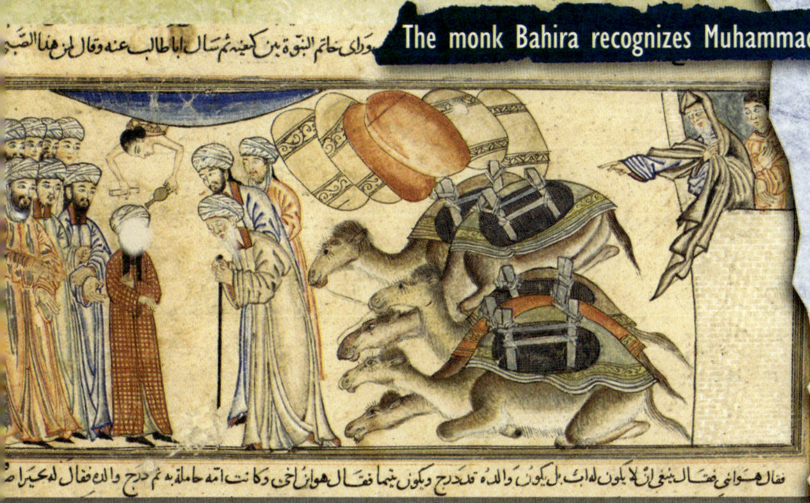
The monk Bahira recognizes Muhammad.

The angel and his words were on every horizon. Muhammad had to face the vision and message no matter where he turned. At first, Muhammad did not accept what he was seeing and hearing. He was troubled by his **revelations**. Yet, he could not help but pay attention to the voice. A change soon came over him. The change Muhammad experienced would change the world.

Muhammad's wife, Khadijah, was among the first to hear about the information the angel revealed to Muhammad. She listened, questioned, and then accepted what Muhammad said as true. However, Muhammad was unsure what to do next, especially since the angel stopped coming to him. Sometimes, Muhammad doubted what had happened. He began to wonder if he was **insane**, or losing his mind. He was confused and felt very alone.

## Led by Light

In another story, young Muhammad was traveling in a **caravan**, or a group of travelers. A monk saw a cloud above the caravan. He went to see who was in the caravan. The monk saw a special sign between Muhammad's shoulders. The monk said the mark meant Muhammad was special.

## Muhammad's Heart

There are stories that tie Muhammad's childhood to angels. One story says that angels visited Muhammad while he was with the Bedouins in the desert. The angels opened his chest and removed Muhammad's heart. They took a black spot from it and then put it back. This story supports the belief that Muhammad lived without **sin**.

the Qur'an

## Well Versed

The loneliness Muhammad felt came to an end when the angel began to reappear. Muhammad became convinced that **judgment day** was coming. He decided that it was his duty to tell people about his revelations. They needed to surrender to God and live their lives a new way.

Muhammad started by speaking with those closest to him. One of his slaves was among the first to believe him. Muhammad's cousin, Ali, decided to support him as well. Soon, other cousins joined in and took part in the discussions. The revelations that he shared with them were eventually written down and became the **Qur'an** (kuh-RAHN).

As time went on, Muhammad shared what he was being told with others. Some people believed what Muhammad was saying. He soon had his own followers. This group of family and friends became the first Muslims. But not everyone believed Muhammad. Many traders were opposed to Muhammad's revelations. They were afraid of **monotheism**. That is the idea of one God. This would scare away people from other tribes who came to do business with them.

Nonbelievers throw stones at Muhammad.

## Judgment Day

The Qur'an, like the Christian Bible, talks about a future day of judgment. In Islam, everyone who ever lived will be resurrected, or raised from the dead, on judgment day. The Qur'an says that only those who believed in Muhammad's revelations and did good deeds will go to heaven.

## Nonbelievers

Most people in Makkah did not believe Muhammad. The idea of a judgment day did not make sense because they thought that death ended everything. To try to get people to think about an all-powerful God, Muhammad pointed to nature. He asked them to see the wonders there.

# The Turning Point

## Death and Beginnings

The year 619 was a turning point for Muhammad. His wife died, and so did the uncle and clan leader who had protected him. Yet the revelations continued. It was about this time that an angel appeared and took Muhammad on a journey. Muhammad rode on a magical creature with wings. The animal, called the *Buraq* (BOOR-ahk), took him to the top of a temple in Jerusalem.

This temple is also thought of as a mountain. Sometimes, it is described as a wall. From this spot, Muhammad was taken through hell. Then, he went through seven levels of heaven. Hell was a place of punishment. Heaven was a place of wonder and reward. An angel guarded each level of heaven. At each level, a **prophet** spoke to Muhammad. At the end, Muhammad stood before God.

By that time, Muhammad was sharing his revelations with a wider audience. Many people in Makkah and beyond talked about him. The number of his followers grew. However, his ideas were not fully accepted by everyone. His beliefs angered many people. Within each family, there were those who followed his thinking and those who liked the old beliefs.

Muhammad rides the Buraq to heaven.

## Prophets

Many religions feature stories about prophets. In religion, prophets sometimes serve as messengers from God, telling people what God has to say to them. Other times, prophets foretell, or predict, future events. In Islam, prophets spoke to Muhammad to bring him special messages from God.

## Older Revelations

In Islam, people believe that there were prophets who came before Muhammad who had received revelations. However, the people who passed down the older revelations changed them, so the meaning changed. The revelations received by Muhammad are thought of as final. They are considered perfect.

## The Hijrah

Makkah was becoming more dangerous for Muhammad and his followers. Not everyone accepted Muhammad and his revelations. Many people **persecuted** him and his followers. They made sure Muhammad knew that he was unwelcome in Makkah. At about this same time, the people in Medina were looking for a leader. A big change was about to take place.

Medina was built on an **oasis**. This means that the land in that part of the desert was very **fertile**. The clans and people from different religions that had settled there were all fighting. The troubles were hurting the town. In 620, Muhammad met with representatives from Medina. They wanted him to go to their city and work out a peace agreement. To get him to go, they signed a **pledge**. In the pledge, they promised Muhammad that they would welcome his followers.

That same year, Muhammad told his people to go to Medina. About 70 of them made the move. The timing was important. Muhammad's enemies were planning to kill him. He escaped from Makkah just in time. This move from Makkah to Medina is called the **Hijrah** (HIJ-ruh). The year 622 is now thought of as year one in the Islamic calendar.

Muhammad and followers flee from Makkah to Medina, pursued by enemies.

Muhammad gives orders to build the Mosque of Medina.

## To Makkah

After the Hijrah, Muhammad received another revelation. He told his people to turn to Makkah to pray. Muslims still turn toward Makkah to pray.

## Man of the People

Muhammad was considered a prophet, but he was also seen as a skilled politician. He was asked to go to Medina in order to get the people to work together rather than fight. He helped develop a constitution in which the groups that were fighting agreed to give one another rights.

## The Battle of Badr

After the move to Medina, the Muslim soldiers started **raiding** caravans. This was a way to provide for their families and to show their power. In 624, Muhammad was informed that the Quraysh, the ruling tribe of Makkah, was sending 1,000 soldiers to attack Medina. Muhammad could only send 313 of his own men. The two armies met at a place called Badr (BAD-er). Even though they were outnumbered, the Muslims won the Battle of Badr.

The Quraysh was now determined to destroy Muhammad and the Islamic community in Medina. They sent 3,000 soldiers to fight the Muslims in Medina. In 627, Makkah sent another 10,000 soldiers to Medina. However, the Muslims dug a large ditch around their city. The **invaders** could not cross the ditch and were unable to defeat the Muslims. This was called the Battle of the Trench.

the Battle of Badr

Abu Bakr (standing) mourns the death of Muhammad.

In the following years, Muhammad tried to claim Makkah's shrine as a place of Muslim worship. He met with the city's leaders and made agreements with various groups. During this time, Muhammad's people grew in numbers. In 632, Muhammad finally led his people into Makkah.

Muhammad died soon after on June 8, 632. Abu Bakr (ah-BU BA-kuhr) became the new Muslim leader.

## The First Four

The leaders who followed Muhammad's death are called the Rightly Guided **Caliphs** (KAL-ifs). Abu Bakr was the first. He was part of the Quraysh and was one of the first to follow Muhammad. Abu Bakr was helped by Umar (OO-mahr), who was the second leader. When Umar was murdered, Uthman (ooth-MAN) took over. When he was killed, Ali became the leader.

## In the Family

After the first four leaders, there was a period in which **dynasties** ruled. This means that leaders passed their power to family members. From 661 to 750, the Umayyad (oo-MAHY-ad) dynasty ruled. The Abbasid (uh-BAS-id) dynasty then ruled from 750 to 1258.

# The Sacred Scriptures

a Qur'an school in Palestine

The Qur'an is the core of Islam. It is said to have all the knowledge a Muslim needs to live a virtuous life. The Qur'an contains the words, or sacred scriptures, of God as revealed to Muhammad through the angel Gabriel. The Qur'an is written in Arabic. Arabic is the sacred language of Islam.

There is no beginning, middle, or end to the Qur'an. Its sections are arranged much like a spider's web. The Qur'an has 114 sections called ***suras*** (SOOR-uhz). Each sura has verses. The longest sura has 286 verses. The shortest has three. The longer suras come first. All suras, except for one, open with, "In the Name of God, the Infinitely Good, the All Merciful."

It is said that there were several versions of the Qur'an at the start, but the third caliph gathered them all together to create the official version that is followed today.

The sayings from Muhammad are meant to ring in the ears of his followers from birth to death. A baby's father whispers words of the Qur'an when the child is born.

Qur'an students in Turkey

## Signs of Respect

There are many rules that must be followed to show respect for the Qur'an. Among them, people are to face Makkah when saying their prayers. They should clean their hands before touching the Qur'an. They should end their prayers by saying, "God the Great One spoke the truth."

## Spoken Word

The word *Qur'an* means "the recitation," or reading. Speaking the words of the holy book is supposed to grant a blessing to the person who says the words and to the people who hear them. Speaking the words is an art form. There are even competitions to see who can do it the best.

a seventeenth-century Qur'an

# The Prophets

People with different beliefs all lived in the same part of the world where Muhammad lived. So Islam, Christianity, and Judaism share many of the same stories. They also share many of the same figures.

Muhammad mentioned prophets found in the Bible. He discussed some of them. Many others were simply named. For example, Abraham, Noah, and Moses appear in the Qur'an, as they do in Christian and Jewish stories. In the Qur'an, these leaders encourage people to use justice when dealing with one another. They tell people to look for a day of judgment. The Qur'an also talks about Jesus. Christians think of Jesus as part of God. Believing in him is said to save people from their sins. However, in Islam, Jesus is seen as a prophet, not a savior.

an image of Jesus from an Islamic text

## Many Names

The name Muhammad means "the glorified one." He is also Ahmad, or "the most glorified." There is also the name Al Mustafa (ahl moo-STAH-fah), or "the chosen one." There are said to be 99 names that honor Muhammad.

## In Action

Like pillars that hold up a roof, Islam has Five Pillars of Worship. They include declaring that there is one God, praying daily, helping the needy, fasting and reflecting, and making a **pilgrimage** to Makkah.

Muhammad and Moses

The Grand Mosque of Makkah

In Islam, Muhammad is not seen as part of God. Muslims do not worship Muhammad in the same way Christians worship Jesus. Instead, Muhammad is seen as a model for living. Muslims try to live their lives as Muhammad lived his.

## The Sunnis

The majority of Muslims are Sunni (SUOON-ee) Muslims. They continue what are considered conventional, or regular, traditions. Some Muslims are also called Sufis (SOO-feez). The Sufis are more **mystical**, or mysterious, in their worship. They dance as a form of spiritual **meditation**.

## The Shi'as

The Shi'as (SHEE-ahz) are Muslims who believe that Ali, who married Fatimah, should have taken over when Muhammad died. They believe that the leadership should come from Ali's family. They place more emphasis on suffering and paying for sin. Some Shi'as believe that Ali had a hidden copy of the Qur'an and knew its true meaning.

## The Final Prophet

People often think about sin. They wonder about evil. In Islam, Muhammad is thought of as being without sin. Muslims believe that God sent thousands of prophets and that Muhammad was the last one. They say he came to correct what was said and believed before.

Many people who think about religion look for signs and miracles. One of the suras says that when Muhammad was born, a light shone throughout the world. It was said to be a reflection of God. Muhammad, however, did not care much for miracles. He said the revelations were all that anyone needed. Even this did not stop his followers from telling wondrous stories about him.

Like all faiths, Islam is about behaviors and beliefs. In Islam, the ways people act are judged by the laws of Islam. People can study the Qur'an to learn how to act. People can also pray to be saved. They can pray for strength.

Shi'a shrine in Iraq

Sunni Mosque in Lebanon

dancing Sufis

# The Sayings of Muhammad

The **hadiths** (hah-DEETHS) are texts about Islam. They are observations about what Muhammad did, said, and saw. The hadiths are meant to guide Muslims. Consider this familiar saying: If you cannot say something nice, then do not say anything at all. Islam has a popular hadith that is similar—If you believe in God and the Last Day, you should say good things or nothing at all.

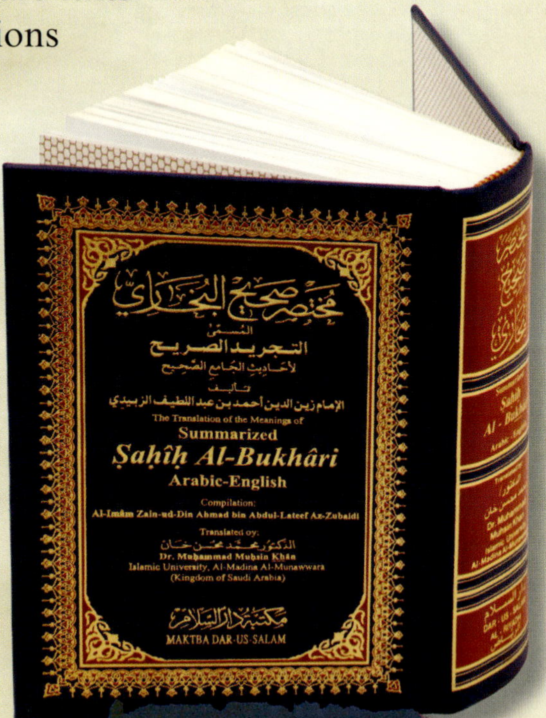

a hadith publication

The importance of a hadith is always measured. People think about who wrote the hadith. They also think about what it means. Some of the observations are more important than others. Each year, more and more people share hadiths.

A man named Muhammad who lived in a desert started Islam long ago. Today, Islam continues to grow. Each day, Islam adds new followers. It is the fastest-growing religion in the world. A community of believers took root many years ago, and like seeds, their ideas spread. The beliefs took hold in faraway places.

Muslims pray in their mosque.

## 40 Hadiths

Today, there are thousands of hadiths. To introduce them, many teachers of Islam use what is called the 40 Hadiths. These are 40 of the most popular sayings. They are typically used when teaching children about Islam.

## Peace Be Upon Him

When the name of a prophet or an angel is spoken, Muslims offer a special saying. In Arabic, it means, "Peace be upon him." When the name Muhammad is spoken, Muslims say something similar, "May Allah honor him and grant him peace."

# Glossary

**ancestors**—the family members that came before you and your family

**Bedouins**—the nomadic tribes of the Arabian, Syrian, and North African deserts

**caliphs**—the Islamic rulers who came after Muhammad

**caravan**—a group of travelers on a journey through a desert

**dynasties**—the lines of rulers that follow from families

**fertile**—producing lots of vegetation or crops

**hadiths**—the literature about the Qur'an

**herders**—people who move animals around in a herd

**Hijrah**—the move the first Muslims made from Makkah to Medina

**insane**—not right in thinking, crazy

**invaders**—the people or other living things that enter an area to take it over

**Islam**—a religion based on the belief in God and Muhammad as God's prophet

**judgment day**—a belief in some religions that there will be a day where one's sins will be judged by God

**Ka'ba**—the holy shrine in Makkah

**meditation**—spending time in quiet thinking

**monotheism**—a belief in one God, as opposed to many gods

**Muslims**—the people who follow the ways of Islam

**mystical**—involving experiences of God that are mysterious or not felt by the usual senses

**oasis**—the green areas in desert regions

**peninsula**—a piece of land that sticks out into water and is nearly surrounded by water

**persecuted**—treated harshly because of one's beliefs

**pilgrimage**—a journey to a shrine or other sacred place

**pledge**—a promise

**prophet**—person who repeats messages they say are from God or a god

**Qur'an**—the holy book of Islam

**raiding**—attacking

**reputation**—the things that are said or believed about something or someone

**revelations**—the communications of divine truth

**shrine**—a place where someone can pray to a deity

**sin**—a moral law created by a religion

**suras**—the common name for the parts of the Qur'an

# Index

# Your Turn!

In 610, Muhammad was a middle-aged man who had grown weary of the harsh world around him. He found solitude in a cave outside of Makkah. It was here that the angel Gabriel was said to have visited Muhammad. This event changed the Arab world. Because of the importance of the event that happened there, Muslims still visit the cave today.

## Life in the Arab World

Make a T-chart. Label the left column "Before Muhammad's Teachings." Label the right column "After Muhammad's Teachings." Then, make a list of details in each column that compare and contrast life in the Arab world.